Wyatt,
You were my first
spark, a little light
my life. I am _so_ glad
get to be a parent to you.

Come Down

I Love You.

Come Down

A Poetic Evolution of the Soul

By: Korynn Amm

Kindle Direct Publishing
2020

ISBN: 978-0-578-72050-0

Printed in the United States of America

First Printing, 2020

This book is dedicated to my dear daughter, Eleanor Rose.

*May you be blessed beyond. May you be encouraged through,
and may you, in this life, organically find you.*

I love you so much.

.

Kissy
Ugga-Mugga
Hugga Hugga.

Love,

Mommy

Not everything is black and white

Once you start seeing the depths in color
Your soul ignites
And that, my friends, is something
Even the strongest, most stubborn souls
Cannot fight.

So take a read with me,
Allow your soul to see
The world,
Your world,
Differently,

Come down,

Heal.
With
Me.

Table of Contents

Lost in a Piece of Paper (Again)

I'm not sure where this is going to take me....
Words with expression.
Writing my confession.
Wondering through depression.... nah.
Just trying to make the best of the worst parts of me
Trying to laugh, when I want to cry
Trying to hang out, when I'd rather hide
Trying to stay, when I should just say good bye
Trying to pray, but I can hardly close an eye
It's just one big lie.

Because honestly,
I'm tired of it all
And I just trip myself until I fall
Or I'm pressed against a wall
Crawl out... but I stall
Wait, hesitate.
Try to recommunicate
What I want you to appreciate
And every time I leave,
...devastated

Must have miscommunicated
Or maybe you never appreciated
And I would not be separated
Jaded.
Degraded.

Trying to find my exit now.
Sitting in a pew, head bowed
Searching, but staring at the floor
Head in hands, heart is sore
Tears splash my knees,
Wanting some release,
But all I can say is please,
Please.
Praying, please.

I've never been right here before.
I don't know what to do.
praying..... please.....
And trying to get back in tune.
Praying, please.... soon.
Opening my eyes, having dealt with what's inside
Drying up my tears, and having nothing left to hide
Standing straight back up,
I know what I must do.
Pray, say please, good bye
There's nothing left for you
And all that's left for me...
Well...
Is hope.

Because I admit to my mistakes
I take full responsibility
And the power is now mine
No more predictability
Sorry-
It's not easy to hear,
Nor is it for me to say
I followed your heart too long,
And now I'm lost, astray

It was your heart that captured me,
Your heart that kept me safe
Your heart that burdened me
And to your heart, I gave
And it was my heart that's broken,
My heart that's bruised,
My heart got stolen, shattered, abused
I'm not saying it was a loss,
Nor am I saying you loved me not,
I'm saying the last petal fell,
And you hurt me a lot
Somehow, my poems, my lyrics or song
Are all about you,
And how things got so wrong

Come Down

So long.

I'm gone.

Convinced myself right
Listening,
Refusing to fight.
Acceptance
A smile
A wave, and a tear
Time to face it all now,
No reason to fear
I could keep writing, about how I have no idea
What's going to come my way,
And what's already here.
I think we can agree,
This is how it should be
Clearly,
I see.
You're free
Reality
Sets me to be me
And no longer as we
Can we separately be?
I guess we will have to see
Because this is how it is now
Somehow,
And who would've thought

I don't know how to end this,
I'm not sure how this works.
I guess just have to work things out
Even if it hurts.

A Poetic Evolution of the Soul

I'll end it on this note
Please just let this go
I don't know how to talk about this,
It's just how I feel

How I sort out all my thoughts
I'm tired of how we try and try
And always get in knots.

I'm tired.
You're tired.
Let's just give it a rest
And if it slips into a coma   Without
It's for the best   Within
Praying... please...   Again
Please.   Sin
Release.   In
Relief.   When
Relive.   Where
Alive.   There
Live.   Here
Love.   Hear
Above.   Him
Enough.   He
It's tough.   In
The thought.   I
Throughout.   .

Out of Touch

Out of touch in my expression
Clear my fear
Give me some refreshin'
Wipe my tear
Hear my confession
And help me steer
Let me be a blessin'
Let me hear
Something real

I've lost my touch   I can feel it
I've lost my way   I can see it
I'm losing my gripping
And I've been tripping
Lost my footing
But I kept going
To where?

Sometimes, I worry what they think about me
Too much
Sometimes, I am scared of their questions
That I won't have all the right answers
Scared of their judgements
That I won't live up to it

Even now, as I write
What will they think of me?
When I see them
Will they ask me?
Are they going to talk about this?

Trying to be vulnerable, but keeping my guard up still
Trying to be real, but hiding behind a masquerade
Trying not to give up on what I know to be Truth

Hey, I'm just being honest.
I don't have it all together.
I'm not trying to be modest

I'm just trying.

Same as you.

That's all I have.

Maybe I'll get back to it later.

The Ocean

Have you ever seen it?
An ocean so blue
So inviting
With its wonderous waves
crashing into the shore.

The view.

Have you ever been in it?
Chills, up your spine,
The hesitation
The anticipation
The chilling sensation
Surrounding your body,
Submerging you with everything it has to offer.

Have you ever gone under?
The blurred vision lens,
When you can't breathe at all
And your muscles start to tense
Does it make sense?

Have you ever gave in?
To an ocean so blue,
As blue as the sky...
On a hot afternoon?
Have you?
Well, if you haven't yet,
You might very soon.
Everyone gives into
This Beautiful Sea.

Have you ever seen the bottom?
Of the beautiful hole,

Did you know,
When you're low,
You have no idea where to go.

It's like the lower you go,
The pressure builds up,
Your senses don't make,
Blurred vision, now blank-
Those chills turn to shivers,
The shivers to shakes...

Nothingness.

Feeling around,
To release the mistakes
That are holding you down...

It's almost over.

With every air bubble
Released,
Getting harder to breathe,
And nothing you see.
Nothing you see.

Confess to the black
With the air you have left
You will be forgiven.
Released from the death.

In hoping,
And praying
With everything left
Just scream it all out,
Surrender
Your very

Come Down

Last
Breath

The exit.

Floating with weakness,

The pressure
Released.

Your senses make sense,
Finally.

Relief.

Have you ever seen it
An ocean so blue
So inviting
Be careful
It might swallow you, too.

With This Life

Life right now is an utter mess.
A world I used to try to protect
With beliefs I said
And what I thought,
It never lined up quite,
So I fought
The truth inside
though buried,
It could not hide.

Against the wind
Like a feather being pulled down to the Earth
There was no other way around,
So I gave in

And now
I found
Within
The sound
Of music.

The Great Entrance into life,
The Dream,
Of what we all strive to be
Though we've never seen
What's right in front of us.
Suddenly,
It's clear to me.

That with this life,
I thee wed
To be with me
'Til I are dead.

And since it seems
The path I tread,
Has led me to
the first thing I said.

Come Down

Now, to my Father
I ask of thee,
Forgiveness,
Grace,
Let mercy be.

For now I see,
Not understand?

You, like I, have felt deep pain
We win,
We lose,
But, how, when,
Did it become a game?

And as we reach the finish line,
We cannot go revisit time.
So, I take this wine,
I make a toast,
I try to rhyme,
I try to boast.

That I know best,
Though you know most,
Like the
Father,
Son,
And
Holy
Ghost.

It makes no sense.
Nor does this game-
Winning?
Losing?
I try to tame,
Myself to be
The pawn pieced perfect
Way you see-

Perspective is a man's best friend.
Successful games, without an end.

With better thoughts,
and a clearer mind
It is now
I feel the leash unwind

Relaxed at last,
I rest my head.
And dream of things
I see
Ahead
I take those dreams,
Make those my thoughts.
I take those thoughts,
And make it seem
That everything's
As it should be.

And, again, again
Recycling...
Success for failures.
Walls for doors
Slides for hills
And lights flickering shadows on the floor.
But,
With this life,
I taketh thee,
And vow to make the best of me
For if I don't
I have to blame
Only me and my
Unforgiven shame.

Dreaming now
To wake up later.

Sweet dreams, my Shadow Perpetrator.

When God Gets
Your Heart Racing

Anticipating the adrenaline
Tense
No
Intense
Overwhelmed again.

Perspiration.
Focus.
Distracted again.

First, it's this.
Then, it's that.
It was here.
Now, it's there.

Anxious with anxiety everywhere.
Puddled in my prayer.
Hopping through the hope.
You see,

Hydrated Again.

Agape

A love that's growing fonder.
On my left side, near my heart.
Carved, forever, in my ribs.
Since that's from where I start.

From dust blown around like ashes,
Created me this mess.
But Your unconditional love
Is what makes me truly blessed.

When nothing else can hide me
And I'm feeling the defeat.
This will forever remind me,

Agape.

Love.

Complete.

Misunderstood

Do you agree or disagree with the words that I say?
Just hear me out.
Do you agree or disagree with the way that I pray?
Don't tell me.
Do you agree or disagree with these clothes that I wear,
How I do my hair,
My friends over there?

Well, I think it's unfair...
The way you stare like you really do care,
As your whispers fill the air.

I agree that I, like you, am rare
I need your prayer
But, please, just listen...
Because I'm right here.

Do you understand me?
Let's talk.

And when we do...
Don't try to be right,
I don't want to fight,
Just give you incite,
My perspectives of life,
My emotions,
My belief,
My desires,
My thoughts,
My questions,
My fear,
My God,
Myself.

You don't have to agree,
Because you're missing the point.
I just ask that you be

Then, maybe
You'll understand why I dress the way I do.
Why I do things differently than you.
And, that's the way it is supposed to be.

Many parts,

One Body.

So, please don't judge me by my mistakes.
Better yet
Re-evaluate.
Because we're all hypocrites.
I mean human
Divine inside,
Somewhere.

Trying to figure ourselves out.
Meaning?
Past, why?
Present, how?
Future, when?

When you completely understand you
Then we can sit down,
I'll listen.
You tell me what to do.
Until that non-existing day.
I will pray.

Come Down

That the whispering will fade
And when the words clear,

A New Day.

Praise the Lord!
Forgiveness.
Mercy
Grace.
Amen.

Raindrops, like tears, fall from my eyes
Cleansing my world,
Drenched
Refreshed

The
Sunrise.

Revelation.

Oh to Dream

Just when you think about it
A little too much,
It changes.

Just when you wish for it
With all your heart,
It happens.

Just when you want it to go away
With nothing left,
Not even the memories,
It appears.

The Circle of Life.
Look, it's right here.

Is this the way it's supposed to be?
This dog-eat-dog world reality.

Needing a change right now,
Trying to sleep.

Forgetting,
Forgiving,
Regretting,
Reliving,
Trying to dream.

Who

Cares.

Caught.
Dead in my tracks.

Tracing them back

Come Down

To where I've been,
I've been here before.

Pressing on to new grounds,

Who

Cares.

Exhausted.

Needing to dream a little more.

I'll go lay my head on the pillow
The one that's there every night
Caressing my cheek as I wonder at the sight.
And the blanket that brushes my shoulder
Comforting me to sleep
Dreaming.
I might…

It's relieving
Believing
Tomorrow can change
Achieving new things,
I'm-possible,
The rearrange,
Yet, somehow
Deceiving-
It has to be right.
It has to be possible.
There has to be light.

Otherwise, what's in a dream?
A lost hope?
Is there such a thing?

Broken Promises

Surrounded

Alcohol and cigarettes
All of these damn regrets
Waking up in Sunday's Best
Living life like all the rest
No regrets

Broken Promises

Solitude

Waiting around for your call
Thinking,
Staring blankly at the wall
I thought I heard you
Hesitate,
You stall
And now, again,
Here comes the fall

Broken Promises.

Reading letters that you wrote
Asking questions, I could quote
Listening to promises that you broke
Broken record, such a joke

Excuses.

Caring nothing, how I feel
Everything is so surreal
But, is anything even real
Can a broken spirit heal
I just can't deal

And so I kneel

Come Down

Broken Promises

I have given you my word
As you have given yours
A love that, forever, will endure
Yet, both our hearts
Still sore

Broken Promises

You'll keep your word,
If I'll keep mine
But to me, yours is greater
Standing the test of time,
For my few words are far between
Speechless, I'll tell you later
Broken Promises
Eye deep in lies
I lie beneath
A bed of false forgiven truths
I weep

And nothing I feel lately
If only I could see
The proof of Truth-
I did.
Beyond,
Your
Broken Promises.
What's it going to take.
To make-
Well, that was a stupid mistake
I take
It back,
For your sake
Am I a fake?
I need to awake.

Healing hopes to unhide the hurt.

I'd like that
A sense of forgiveness
That comes from the dirt.

East to the West
Release from the stress
Forgetting those regrets

I'd like that

Tomorrow.

On the Brighter Side

Dealing with the reality
Things aren't always what they seem
People change,
And in the end it's for the best.
Relax.
Rest.

Breathe in,
Take in
Everything

There's purpose
Behind it all

Somewhere

Open your eyes
Look within
Inside there are mirrors reflecting
Deflecting
Obsessing over the things they say
The way they treat you
The lies they pray
Don't listen to them

Anyway

There is a way to look within
Adjust
Align
Dig deep and shout
And pray without
Resistance
Again and again

Until

You soak it in.

A Poetic Evolution of the Soul

Take it in.
Believe that
Again and again

This world has so much to offer
Take it as it comes to you,
Believe what you know
And remember to grow
Don't get stuck in the middle.
Or at the ends
Broaden your horizons
And don't forget to watch the sunrise each day
That's the hope to hold on to
The gift that is given to you
Take it in
Believe that

Share your heart
And don't give yourself away
Unless it's solely your choice
That's the beauty of this game
And never
Let anyone
Ever
Take anything away from you
Ever.

It's yours to give
Don't let people mistreat the way you live
Disrespect you
Bring you down
After all
It is your life
Love it

Again and again

Say what you mean
And mean what you say
Every day

Come Down

Live with your heart
Not just with the time you have today
And make time
Because once time changes
It's hard to put it back together
The pieces will never fit the same once
They're severed

Again and again

Look around
Look inside
That's life
Breathe it in
Take it in
And remember
Believe that

It's all you got.

Part One

Confession-
So captivating
The truth will set you free.

Direction-
So hesitating
Unsure of where I'm meant to be.

I feel
And to feel anything tonight
Would help me sleep tight.
It's real.

Thirsty for so many things,
Answers,
Water,
Living.
Draining so much right now,
Tears,
Pains,
Emotions, run down.
A blink of Hope between the tears-
I feel You here,
I feel You here.

Don't let me forget
Already regretting the moment
When I release it-
Agape.

Come Down

Let my faith stay tonight,
Beyond this world,
This hopeless swirl,
The battle of this fight-
Let my actions scream
Beyond my words,
Let my love cast
Beyond my worries,
Let my energy jump
Past my regret,
And let me believe that.

Will it here.
Not selfishly to mend my own despair,
That seems…
Who cares.
Paying it forward,
Putting it back out there.

For them,
For us,
For me to share.

Part Two

You are in the storm.
The rain kisses my cheeks,
The lightning strikes my eye,
The thunder rolls, and pulses me
In this storm across the sky.

You are here.

I feel you through my fingers,
Your Spirit clasps my hand,
As I travel right on through You,
I breathe you in again.

Remembering,
I've been here before.

The clouds release their tears
Splashing down onto my cheeks
Mixing with my fears
Puddles the ground beneath my feet.

My thoughts jump around
Like lightning bolts
They streak
Flash
Beauty
Boom
Igniting me somewhere deep inside
I'm running out of room.

Remembering.
Remembering,
I've been here before.
The thunder beats to the beats
Of my ever, unsteady breath
Just breathe
Wait and rest

Come Down

In this moment,
Find your breath
Releasing
Just observe
As the storm rolls in
Then out
Refreshed with tears
Released
My world is hydrated again.
No doubt.
Rays beam through the darkest clouds
Shining deep on past the grey.
Bringing pulse and promise to the heart
And beauty to this storm
And the rainbow is the natural art
Of how we are transformed

Enjoy
This perfection
To realize
What I lack
Repeat

Part Three

I am guarded.

Because I am scarred
Because I thought I knew
But as I see you there
A fence rises around this room
This heart of mine
Can't bloom
The rising walls painted in white lies
Blue tears fill the skies

Guarded, I walk in this desert place,
Searching for this thing called

Amazing Grace?

So I can forgive and cut the vines
That covers this face
And makes my heart blind.

I am guarded.

Part Four

Poetry is.

Every moment is poetic in
life.

Poetry captures
The nature of this world.
Both
Hellish and Heavenly.
Always
Bringing hope
Releasing fears
And tears.

Like a rain cloud rolling in,
Poetry is
Loud.

But like the breeze,
Sometimes
Poetry is
Just a feeling.

Poetry is.

Like the air,

Sometimes
There wouldn't be
Life
Without it.

It is
darkness
But it brings
Light

With each line
Releasing

Poetry is
Love.

A Flustered Clustered N.O.T.E.

I love the power I have with words
But I'm careful with what I say

Words can
cut
so
d
  e
    e
      p.

Just listen to me here.

Poetry is the best way for me to describe what's on my heart.
Because I don't have a backbone to speak my mind.
You hear?

I don't want to hurt everyone's feelings all the time,
Or is that just me?

Tired of being hurt.
Keep going.

I
Will
Write
My
Backbone

Because
Once
I was scarred with words
That were lies.

And
Now
If you read this willingly
It is your choice to take to heart what you want.

Come Down

Trying to find my own path
Aside from the dreams I had
Aside from the path they took when they made the right choices
Where is the rule book,
Why aren't you following it?
Because I am not who I was
I am not them
So listen up
And
Get a grip of something else!

I'm well,
Sure
I could be better
So could you
I'm working on it-

I'm trying

But with you coming in and out
Being this person then that
Here then there
I'm crazy.
Crazy for the person I think you might be,
And crazy for the person that I long to be.
It doesn't make any sense
You're telling me!

Read on.
Because if you want to know my heart,
My heart is this-

Sacrifice

If I've learned one thing-
Agape,

It's Love.

A Poetic Evolution of the Soul

And I feel like I'm losing a grip of something here again.

I have been here before
I don't know what it is,
It's sore.

This is everything I have in one big N.O.T.E.
(never.orally.tell.everything)

Some things are okay left unsaid
I guess.
Always being hushed
I write away my stress.

Don't go around breaking things just because you can.
Pray.
And pray a lot

Love will happen,
Just be
Patient for it

You really should be looking for it instead of looking at me.
Preparing to be open to it-
Don't close up again.
You'll see.

And for you with the unwashed hands,
If you only knew the damage a little dirt can do,
It goes a long way...
Get a grip on reality, too.

Scum.

It makes people numb.

Stop making excuses
Just do what you say
And say what you're going to do.

Come Down

Show a little more love
Because it'll go a long way
And give people hope
Don't lead them astray.

I feel like I should delete
Everything I just wrote
Pretending it was never felt,
Laugh it off like it's a joke.

Worried for who will read this-
What will they say?

But
I'm not going to
Right here is where it will stay.

You willingly read it,
You can willingly take
to heart what resonated with you.

It's poetic.
The connections.

And who knows,
It may not have made any sense,
That's fine
I just needed to vent.

And here's my voice in a N.O.T.E.

Give me a chance to show you who I have become,
I won't be a disappointment,
I won't let you down

Not like everything else has

A Poetic Evolution of the Soul

I am different.
You knew that from the beginning.

I love the power I have with words,
But I really don't speak my mind because I am afraid.

If I may,
Actions speak louder
than any word can ever say.

And right now, it seems like one big act,
Trying to keep things intact...
Barely, and that's a fact.
You and I both know that.

The greatness beyond the things you will never understand
And the pain and confusion you have placed in my hand
Is a blessing in disguise and is unfolding a new plan

Keep hope
Find love
And share both with us all
Hold onto to the Faith
And prepare for the Fall.

Forgive those who need it
They know not what they do
Move forward and see it
The future set for you.

And through the fear you
Must pursue.

Love with your heart
Not with your mind
Release all the lies
While there's still time.

Come Down

Please do not wait
Don't hesitate
Because by then
It might be too late

Enjoy each day
That's been given to you
And remember there are still some things you can do.

So never forget the power of words,
How actions speak truer than
The words unheard

I love you.

Tense in Every Sense

All it is,
this whole thing
A blast from the past
I just want to move on
But I'm time traveling in reverse.
Get a grip and loosen up!

First I'm not enough
Then, I'm too much
First I'm too soft
Then, I'm too tough

I just don't get it.

I could scream with all the words you say,
With the way you make me feel every day.
I could turn and look at the ground,
Pretend like nobody's around.
Focusing on everything,
Picking apart the smallest thing,
Tearing down my very being
I'm not this or that
Too much here
Not enough there.
Should've been
Could've been
You wish you had
Could've had

I know it's sincere,
It's just not clear
To me.
What to be

It's just pushing me away.

I'm frustrated all the time,

Come Down

But I put my tail between my legs,
Everything is fine.

I can't unwind!
And then you go and change your mind!
Time

After

Time

Don't blame yourself
Because your whole life you have-
For the things that went bad
And now-
I find myself doing the same
Have you ever thought there doesn't need to be a blame?

It's a shame.

I just wish you would see
Just see me.

I really do try-
To do everything right,
I know that I can't
So sometimes I ask myself-
Why
Even
Try

Whenever something goes wrong
The story just goes on.

I just want it to end right there.
Stop!

Worrying so much.
Controlling who I am.
Hesitating,

Perspiring,

Miscommunicating,
because it is annihilating.

Let go.
Let me.
Just be.
You'll see.

Tiny Blossom

Tiny little blossom,
Blowing in the wind.
Why are you so carefree?

Growing in the sunlight,
Drowning in the rain,
Trying so hard to catch a ride
With the free breeze.

Tiny little blossom,
It is time for you to bloom,
You are dancing in this hurricane,
If you don't stop spinning,
Very soon
You'll miss it.

You are just like dust in the wind,
As you frolic about.
There is much now that you doubt.
Maybe gone tomorrow,
You need to ground yourself,
To rid you of your sorrow.
You are like dust in the wind.

Dancing with the leaves,
Feeling great within the breeze.
Living life with this pretend filled ease-
Will only lead,
to death, you see.
You really need to plant that seed.

When I calm this storm,
I take away the sticks and stones,
Will you settle down your petals,
So we can see the beauty in your bones?
Because, Baby Bloom,
I tell you
It was I who planted thee,

So I know what you have been through
Now
Let me tell you what I see.

The beauty, it is truly,
The Greatness that's inside.
The red and pink petals power
Up that twinkle in your eye.

Baby Bloom, once you've blossomed,
Found your truth and let things be,
You'll be settled, grounded, strong
Like the biggest, wisest tree.

Your nectar will be as sweet as the sun that's shining down.
Your fragrance will be wrapped around,
Around, around, around
Attracting all the pollen seeds that drift inside your reach, spreading
love to other Baby Blossoms
Convincing them to find the Ease.

Turning the Page

Turning a new page
Great things have happened
But greater things await.

New horizons with new colors that I have never seen,
Although it seems,
A bit oddly-

I've been here before.
Remembering…

Places that I've never been
Recognize all the beauty
All over again.
Deep within.
Though far away
I came back in.

I've
been
here
before.

This will be the first day of the rest of my life,
Everything, I just know it
Is going to be alright.
The sun will shine bright,
And, late at night,
I can finally rest tight.

See
My callused feet and hardened heart
Where I've been treading
Back and forth
Constantly regretting
Forgetting
Where is North.

Through fear, I pulled my wings apart,
The wind has brought me in this art
Of digging deep to rise up strong,
Accepting all the wrong
That lead me here to write this
song on paper.

Have a little faith,
Even just mustard seed,
Then, let the tears of heaven
Quench you as you need.
And don't forget to read.

Everything rides on hope now,
I'm going to be protected, somehow.
And if this all should fall to the ground,
Your love will set me free,
You just have to believe
That.

Empty Pockets

I used to wear holey jeans
Letting change slip through the cracks.
Getting a stain on my knees
Then dusting off my slacks.

I was allowing my life to live itself
Like a passenger on the train,
Just waiting for the next stop
Until I lost myself, again-
In a N.O.T.E.
that slipped out of that pocket.

Little did I know, how broke I was
Or was going to be.
I was afraid of what I would see,
When all I have,
is nothing.
And nothing is all I have.
Literally.

With empty pockets,
I contemplate
Exhausted myself
I stare at this plate I made it for myself

And I don't even know how to cook.

Graduation finally
From the Clean Plate Club,
Noticeably
The amount of crumbs that I needed to scrub,
Beginning to slowly pick up my own mess,
Slowly relieves a little more the stress.

With my empty pockets,
I will accept
But please expect,
Nothing less

The a perfectly imperfect
Mess.
And Breathe
Within the holes,
There is a Whole.
New me.
The best way to mend,
is to start from within.

So,
I stand here,
in my holey jeans,
with my empty pockets,
staring back at me-
and an open heart,
and nothing, no one here with me.
But I ask the mender to help with these tears,
And piece me back together,
After all of these years-
Tailor made,
flares.

Anxiety

Anxiety can be a debilitating or a driving force in your life.
It depends on how your winds blow.
It depends on where your North Star is.

What is guiding you?

It depends on how you read those around you,
but more on how well you read yourself.

Surround yourself with light because at the end of the day, the
struggles have to be worth something.

Make it all count.
Strive to be lighter, to be the star in someone's night sky.
When you're struggling with anxiety, make it matter.

Make it drive you straight to the source.
Make it look at your fear in the face.

Then, sit in that pocket for a minute
and look at the possibilities.
Notice how your body is reacting, and where this force is driving
you.
Will you choose to believe that fear, stay stuck with it, or learn
from it.

You've been here before.

Morph it into positive action.
Eventually, enough positive actions will seep into your soiled skin
that you will begin to bear your own fruit.
Nurture those fruits.
Grow those fruits.
Share those fruits.

Because if you don't, then what's the reason for any of it?

Anxiety is just a deep seed.
It pushes through those dark times like a weed
That finds a crack in the sidewalk.
It's a driving force to help you become what you were made to be.
Grow.

Painted Pretty

Painted pretty little pictures as we prance
On through this life, we dance
We learn, we try- the chance
That one day it will come to this
We've been entranced…
Complaining constant of the nerve
Of this or that, we swerve
To duck, to run, to dodge, we take
The easiest, quickest, shortest-

We make
It work.
Enough
Is what it never is
Enough of that
Enough of this
Complain we're tired
And sick and tired
And sick of it
Enough

We try
We try to make it right
We try and then put up a fight
Within
Again
We cry and try
And push it down
And fight the time
Complaining something isn't right

We say we try
But then ask why
We don't have time

For this or that
It's a never-ending time warped map
Of life
It hits us in the face
The space that we all try to save
To paint the pictures that they've made
Of us
Enough

The Shift

Tired of trying to do what's right
Color in the lines
Don't keep my face like that for too long
Or I'll go blind?
Something like that-
I couldn't see anyway
With your whole, "Do as I say
Not as I do,"
Staring right back at you
As you project your fears
To steer me clear
From repeating history

You say I have changed a lot-
And I say,
I hope so
Because a lot has changed me.
Instead of forcing all these old ways
Keeping your history at bay-
Always saying, 'Okay,'
So the boat wouldn't rock-
Nobody likes the waves.

Nobody likes the waves.

I'm starting to just let it be
I'm starting to just finally breathe-
On my own,
Without the reliance of your advice nagging
In my head,
Over and over again
Until…

Breathe.
I realize-
I am not the you that you constantly
Projected out of fear that I would turn out to be,
Preventing me from the history.

And now, you see-
This is me.

Forging this new path,
Healing all the wounds from our ancestral past-
Healing is the hardest part,
To admit,
To not quit,
To push through and really feel all of it-
Not shove down and pretend everything is perfect.

I am not him.
I am not her.
I was never going to be that anyways,

I always knew that.
But I tried-

So hard-
To fit in,
To pray right,
To whisper softly so we don't fight.
The waves are rolling in on life-
On mine
On yours
On his
On hers.
You asked for this
I'm just letting it be

For me
For them
New history

Feather-Breathed

A tiny seedlet in the wind,
You came in
When you came in.
Riding on the breeze,
You blew
Gently,
Softly in you flew.
You land gentle on rugged ground,
Seemingly,
Nobody found
Quietly waiting, you drifted by
Keeping to yourself while riding high.

Without a doubt, a thoughtless thought:
This must be all life's really got…

The wind, it blew you, shifting around
The wind, it kept you off the ground
For now,
Tiny little Feather-Breath,
Your shallowness,
Take deeper breaths.

Come down.

Deep within,
Deeper still,
To fill your journey up with hair
Don't just ride this breeze,
Create your will,
Exhale then…
Be still.
Be still.

You've been here before.

A Poetic Evolution of the Soul

You know when it comes,
The push and the shove.
The answers within,
They come from above
Below
Dig down deep,
Ground through your roots,
Deep yet, still, Feather-Breath,
This is your Truth.

Without is where you choose to go?
The doubt is all you'll ever know.
Light as a feather,
Yet
Still as a board.
You doubts create these knows-
Your thoughts just hoard.

Collecting consciousness, you know
It's true.
That nobody, right here, quite
Understands you.
But do you?

Deep within
Deeper still
Fill your journey up with air
Look out, Look up, Look deep inside
This is where the Truth resides.

To ground yourself and lose the chains,
Reveal, sit with and *feel* those pains.
And breathe.

The quietness is where you can hear your soul begin
to sing.

Come Down

Notice
Listen
Accepting
Observe
Move along,
Steady now,
Persisting

Breathe
So you don't swerve
Away and dodge the shadows
They bring to you deep healing
Deep healing.
Shift your sands,
Time is all we have.
The tides are flowing, going,
You are not.

You came in a tiny seed,
And a tiny seedlet you will be
Until,
Replanted,
Refresh,
and Spread to share.

Breathe, and bridge, and be the one
Because there is none like you

Under this sun.

Root to Rise

Rooting down.

Take a breath,
Digging past the clay and crust
Find the source, inside the dirt,
Red layered, dry, unsoiled dust
Safely-
Finding who you are.

Keep digging still.

On towards your core
The mantle's where your pleasure's stored.
Ignite the little orange flame
Accepting them and how they came
Into your life, there is a reason.
A lesson learned for just that season.

Keep digging still.

To find your center,
Accept your truth,
It is your mentor.
Do not doubt yourself this way,
At your core- come what may
This little yellow-littled path
You've root down
To yourself
At last.

Now.

Take
A
Breath
And ricochet

Come Down

Back through the path that you just made.
To bridge your roots up with your heart,
This is where the journey starts.

Lay down
Relish in the green
To understand your own belief
Look up, the love, accept the peace.

Then
Breathe.

Keep floating up into the blue
Acknowledging what is your truth
Speak up, Speak louder for all to hear
Then

Keep floating up
Release the fear.

Ascending to the purple haze
The Galaxy-Releasing Phase
Releasing for your eyes to see
The giftedness inside of thee-

The twinkles diamonds in the sky,
White lights igniting new insights

So

Journey down to come back up
Root down
Breath and listen up
Within yourself
Down to your core

Grounded

Rooted

Connect

Soar

It is the only way to take

But

The choice is only yours to make.

Keep going,
Go on,
Journey through
Begin to see what life
Brings to you.

Stay open.

Connecting the Outlets

The inward gust of wind inside
Your sunrise eyes opened the skies
A brand new day when you were born
Come what may
Completely adorned
You've been here before.

New rhythm, your heartbeat added waves
Vibrating
New pulses into each day
Wired
So tightly, the intricate way
Defining yourself on this path you create

Plugged into your family
Taming your truth
You actions, thoughts
Worth and beliefs about you.

You, innocent one, know nothing at all,
You plugged into this outlet so you wouldn't fall.
Supported and loved, you take it all in
The truths here, you learned, are rooted within
Dear child, keep searching but do not unplug
It's a series, this lifeline that you came into
With love.

Your energy matters
When the circuits connect
The lights, when they're lit,
What a beautiful set
Understandings and truths
You just have to travel

Through these outlets, Soul Spirit,
It's time to unravel
Yourself to the world.

Plugging in now, right onto the next
Relationship wise, it's like the next test
You begin to compare
It opens your eyes
Making you question your truth might be lies.
Plug in and question, create that next layer-
Of a truth that's more *you*, one you'd want to share.

It's not wrong, it's just different, accept it
Because they...
Just like you, they were tamed,
Maybe stuck in their ways.

Don't unplug it completely
From that *family-ar* truth
Connecting these outlets
Is what you do.
Connect them and blend
Become more aware
Watch and they watch you
In awe, they will stare.

Keep going.

Come Down

Your energy matters
When the circuits connect
The lights, when they're lit,
What a beautiful set
Understandings and truths
You just have to travel
Through these outlets, Soul Spirit,
It's time to unravel
Yourself to the world.

Connecting the series of life
Lines in your life
We've been caught in the webs of half truths
And half lies.
Stretching the truth, creates you to question
Allows you to share only what is perception
A deception of truths that plants a new seed,
The fear it has triggered in you and in me.
Twisting our eyes to see linearly
Confusing these "truths" that keep floating around

Stay plugged in,
Do not charge up.
Get yourself to the ground.

Maybe to unplug here
Is really to plug in
Reset that router
Release
Flow again.

A Sacred Pause.

Recenter deep within,
Yourself
To your core
Releasing the lies of the stories you're told
On repeat
By yourself
You must let it unfold.

Your energy matters
When the circuits connect
The lights, when they're lit,
What a beautiful set
Understandings and truths
You just have to travel
Through these outlets, Soul Spirit,
It's time to unravel
Yourself to the world.

Moving on
Up the outlet
Beliefs
Resetting yourself back to peace.
Your heartbeat slows down as you see
The rhythm vibrating in you
And in me
Find your breath

Your energy's free.

Take a moment to acknowledge that journey deep within
The outlets you've connected, where your truth has always been
Connected to Spirit, God, Divine
The Universal Oversoul, this journey through time

Keep connecting these outlets
Then
Openly share
We are all in the same tether of energy here
Somewhere.

Your energy matters
When the circuits connect
The lights, when they're lit,
What a beautiful set
Understandings and truths
You just have to travel

Come Down

Through these outlets, Soul Spirit,
It's time to unravel
Yourself to the world.

Let if flow.

Speak on up
Time to share
Express with confidence
You feel it here

You've been here before.
Release the fear,
Or sink into it
a little more.

You've created this journey
You've wished for so long
You've figured it out
You have written your song.

It's time to plug in
To get on with the next
It's time to push on
Push up to the next outlet.

Your energy matters
When the circuits connect
The lights, when they're lit,
What a beautiful set
Understandings and truths
You just have to travel
Through these outlets, Soul Spirit,
It's time to unravel
Yourself to the world.

Buzzing on up
You're plugged
You can feel it
It's time to tune intuition

A Poetic Evolution of the Soul

Just peel it all back
Show this rhythm of change
Rewired
Not tired
Intricately rearranged
They line up to go out
The go out from within
Bridge the gaps by your breath
Use your gifts for a change!

The finals set in series-
Without doubt
Let's keep going
Is what gets left behind
Time is out
Children knowing
The legacy left in this life
We imprint
On the youth of this world
With a knife we can carve it
Or we can hand it to them

Let them carve for themselves
Their organic, unique wind
To recircle, recycle, reconnect to the start
The beauty to skin is our souls all have art.

Your energy matters
When the circuits connect
The lights, when they're lit,
What a beautiful set
Understandings and truths
You just have to travel
Through these outlets, Soul Spirit,
It's time to unravel
Yourself to the world.

Muddy Waters

Sometimes the hardest thing to do is to embrace the suck.
I suppose a less in your face way to put it would be to get
comfortable in the uncomfortable.

When the going gets tough, it is easy to just get going.
Ignore it.
Shove it down.
Move on.
Shift away from those hard times and pretend that things are fine.
Everything... is... fine.

Fake smile.

Because if things are not fine, there is a problem-
and problems need to be fixed-
and sometimes you just can't fix things.
If it is a problem that cannot be fixed,
then it is easier to ignore said problem
and pretend it does not exist.
Because it will always be a problem
and you will never know how to fix it.
When in fact it is *not* even your problem to begin with.

It makes perfect sense.

Seeded deeply in the soiled soot,
Murky, muddy, sticky place-
Growing slowly through turmoil, but-
Pressing upward, at slow pace.

The timing.

Gritted in the dust and dirt, it's rooted
Strong, this tiny stem,
Searching onward, persisting, resisting still-
Digging deep- some place within.

The process.

The cloudy, darkened waters prove
The beauty that will come-
The petals, once they bloom- you'll see
Why everything was done.

The lotus.

Stillness, Silence and Slowing Down

Stillness is hard.

Silence is awkward.

And slowing down is foreign.

Painting pretty little pictures as we prance
On through this life, this dance
We learn- we try- the chance
That one day it might come to this
We've been entranced.

Complaining constant of the nerve-
Of this or that- we swerve
To duck, to run, to dodge- we take
The easiest, quickest, shortest-
We make
It work

Enough
Is what it never is
Enough of that,
Enough of this
Complain we're tired,
And sick and tired,
And sick
Of it-
Enough
We try
To make it right,
We try and then put up a fight
Within
Again
We try again,
We push it down
And fight this time- within
But time is all we have
Right now

A Poetic Evolution of the Soul

We say we try,
And then ask why, and how...?
We don't have time for this or that
It's a never-ending time-warped map
Of life

And now

It hits us in this place,
To face the time we try to save-
We blink,
And blink, and blink again-
What is happening?

Just breathe...

Look within,
We hold our breath,
Feel our body not at rest,
Our mind is racing-
Worried thoughts,
As our stomach ties in knots

The fear that time is running out,
We're slowing down,
And now we doubt
We don't know how
To slow things down,
Be still, and listen
Root to crown,

Not rooted down,
We fight or flight,
We must learn now-
To make things right
Within, again, we look within
Again, and then-

We're grounded, still-

Come Down

And breathe.

Just like the Spring,
Our growth, it will
Begin to clean,
Begin to still
Our mind because
Now is the time
Because you have the time-
Be still and breathe...

This is not how it will be,
Forever, this will soon be seen-
Remember then-
The pruning clean we made ourselves
Priority.

To purge the old,
Bring in the new-
Decluttered thoughts,
We need more room
Within, again- we can explore
Letting go, and breathing through
The open door of time,
When all you have
Is you.

Time to Till the Soil

Time to till the soil
Where we've settled in our roots
Spring, the sun, is coming soon
Muddy are our boots.
Treading in the trenches,
The constant waterfall of thoughts,
The sun is sending winds of change-
Steady, as we watch.
As history repeats, you see-
The narratives replay,
Our roots are not near as deep
In the soil where they lay.
We feel fleeted,
Near defeated,
As we're forced to quiet down.
Slow down, relax, find the breath- the wind-
It is there we feel the ground.
Time to till the soil
Where we've settled down our roots,
Spring, the sun, is coming soon
Muddy are our boots.
As cleaner water flows, and then it ebbs...
And then it flows-
Time to till the soil- so
The new seeds planted grow.
The sun is sending winds of change-
Steady, as we watch
Muddy boots, our trenches leave
New waterfalls of thought.
It is time to till the soil 'til
This narrative is new.
Rooting down to rise, right now
This wind of change-
It's breathing you.

The Roots

The challenge is to pry it open
Between the fingers
The layers-
It's hidden-
It's deep

The struggle is to continue to pry
Don't lie
Or hide
The struggle is to continue to pry
Just try Keep going, it's deep

The test is that once you're there
To stay and stare
Straight to the fear
Replaying and replaying
From ear to ear
The test is just to stay
Right here

The growth is when you feel the feels
Reliving the real
Sensations- they're real
The deal is when you spin the wheels
Fine tune your feels
Release the fears
Rewrite what plays between the ears
It's just a story you've kept up for years
The growth is when you feel

The question is, "What will you do?"
You face the fear-
Accept the feels-
Begin to finally spin the wheels-
And see that it does not consume you

Right then and there
The question is, "What will you do With that?"

The experience is
That you have yours
And I have mine
And they have theirs
Not wrong or right
The experience is the same
Just In time

The answer is just to trust the fall
Get grounded down
Can't fix it all
Press up again and fix your crown
And use the wall to get grounded down
The rise and fall- we have it all
The ebb and flow
The come and go
The here then there but now quite near
Where we want to be just yet-
You see-
You and me
If we are speaking truthfully
It's clear to see things carefully
That things are usually what they seem
Beating hearts
The river-stream
The flow and go
The rise and fall
The answer is just to trust the fall
Because we all Are
One
One Love
One God
One

Come Down

The funny part of all of it
Is once you start you cannot quit
Because you have awareness lit
Red flame deep in your
Root

Tree Shadow

Supported by the Earth,
Star,
You are supported by the Earth.
Mother grounding you again-
Not far,
We've been connected here since birth.

Supported by your Roots
Tree,
You are supported by your Roots
Absorbing all the ground you feel,
Seed,
You are growing in your truths.

Encouraged by the Sun
Fire,
You are encouraged by the Sun.
Radiate
Follow your desire,
Because we are all here as
One.

Bursting open, watch your buds burst,
Growth,
You are growing in this Rain.
Find the stretch between the Moon and Earth,
Pain,
The space between is where you gain.

Quiet down when there is Nothing,
You will find your True Self there,
Dust,
It has settled, let it be.
Do not judge, allow yourself
To feel the rush.

Come Down

The energy is finally free,
Peace,
Finding balance in what is.
Knowing He in the sky,
Release,
Your fears,
Give them to Him.

Being present is a gift,
Here,
Being called back to receive.
You have always been here waiting,
Dear,
Without explaining,
Let it be.

One Step

Start out slow and find your breath,
You've been here before.
Watch your step.

Then match your breath with every step,
The rhythm of the walk.

Pay attention

Look around-
the sky,
the ground,

Soak it up, let it really surround
You
One step, one breath, one beated path

Pay attention

See if you are paying attention, you won't feel lost because you will
find connections-
The trees, the moss

Some trees are rooted, solid they stand
Observe them, just observe and appreciate the sand
You share with them

Uprooted and fallen, roots mangled underneath
Observe them, just observe and appreciate the soil beneath
That you share with them

Naturally reaching up towards the Sun,
Twisted and tangled, together as one
Tree is needing a little support,
The fallen down trees have created a fort-
Observe them, just observe them and appreciate the Sun
That you share with them

Come Down

Knotted trunk of wisdom gained,
These have been the growing pains-
Released and healed and now can be
Unique marks, the bark, for all to see
The beauty
Observe them, just observe them and appreciate the knots in you
and me

Learn to let go
Of it all
Pay attention
And breathe

One step, one breath, one beated path
Pay attention

Perspective is the perfect way because everyone's is different,
Even though you're the only one that's here
It is apparent-
The signs of life, the dying leaves, and here you are, in between the
tracks that when you look, they lead
You off the path, and that's okay, perspective is the perfect way
That when you come back on this path
You will be reminded that
You've been here before

Pay attention.

Listen.
Pick up the pace,
You found your breath,
Begin to really try and test,
The edge
Of where the growing
Pains
And push the breath into it
Then when the rains
Create the mud,

Slow down to find your step again-
Catch your breath, breathe into it
Just like the trees, they break or bend
Root down, just do it
Do not slip because you do not take
Your hand out for some help,
Mistake.
Climb up the sloppy muddy slope by
Reaching up and out, there's hope.

Find your breath,

You've been here before.

Just

Watch your step.

Come Down

Living our life in the wish they woulds
Know we shoulds
Wish we coulds

Inside with our thoughts
It's time to calm back down
Come back down
Right now

Take a deep breath
To get out of your head
Because you're not really alive
It's time to get out of this bed
You made

Let's connect back through the heart
Then head back to the start
Get your feet on the ground
Right now

Take a deep breath
What is your biggest fear
What gets you back in your head
What makes you get back into bed

What doesn't allow you to feel
What have you been trying to heal
Come on, there's something inside
It's time to open your eyes
And quit repeating those lies
Pretending everything's fine
Wake up

Put your feet on the ground
And stretch the energy up
That has been stuck in the Earth
We are restarting from birth

Connect

Energetically feel,
It's okay- feelings are real
You can allow them to heal,
Begin spinning that wheel
Root down

Take a breath and create it
Manifest with love- how you make it
Connecting up toward yourself
You have ignited the flame

Feel the energy burn,
For years you've tried to just learn-
How to go through the moves,
But you forgot about you-
And that matters.

It's time to find who you are
Who you've been all along
Start loving you for yourself
And all those beautiful scars

Take a deep breath
Time to get out of your head
Root yourself down and stretch out of this bed
Where you've kept yourself safe,
Listening and soaking it in,
It's time to awake
Pay attention

Come down.

Here in Wonderland

Took a breath, closed my eyes
Looked inside, and realized-
Time

The thing that divides us all
Is time

Connecting us, though, Divine
Like the rise of the moon's shine,
The next day- the sun in the sky-
Connected through the passing of time
Took a breath, closed my eyes
Looked inside, watching-
As time just passed me by

Sitting here in Wonderland
Hiding in our rabbit holes
Unearthed, these pathways- The Bigger Plan
Connecting us, to the Oversoul

Connecting through with sympathy?
Sorrowful, it's clear to see
Together we sit comfortably,
Here in Wonderland
Running through our rabbit holes,
Making sure our story's told
Unearthed, these pathways- The Bigger Plan
Is not to just sit
Here in Wonderland.

Connecting through with sympathy
It's easy to get stuck, you see
But as we slowly pick up pace
Admit the fear that's in this place
Begin to stand up in that space
Breathe into it-
It's time to face the fear that's
Here in Wonderland.

And fear is such a funny thing,
Motivating-
When it's shoved down enough, you see-

Energetically,
Ignoring our own truth?
Because, unearthed, these rabbit holes from our youth,
When shoved full with the lies we tell- there's no proof that things
aren't well.
But begin to notice the energy,
As you stand up to the You that you see-
Here in Wonderland.

It's only when you're ready to quit,
Tired, and sick of all of it.
Admit to the Awareness Lamp you lit-
These rabbit holes are meant to connect
Not be filled with dirt,
The hurt- regret-
Not to forget...

But connect.

This is how you will get...
Energy, a breeze, a breath...
Here in Wonderland.
And once you link the fear to feel-
Protected, where you've been for years...
Connections begin to slowly clear
The stagnant air
Here in Wonderland.

Amazed at all the things you passed
Noticing now, these connected paths
These rabbit holes that you shoved down
Are Connected Truths on solid ground
At last
Now sense begins to make
Itself and you can really take
A break

Come Down

A breath
Relaxing
Here in Wonderland.

Embrace the unearthed, deepest roots
Connect yourself back to Your Truth
Connecting now with empathy
I see you now,
And you see me.
Because of all that energy we moved
Here in Wonderland.
A brand new breeze brushes,
Rushes with ease
Breathing into your *dis-ease*
Took a breath, closed my eyes
Looked inside, and realized
Time

The thing that divides us all
Is time
Connecting us though, Divine
Like the rise of the moon's shine,
The next day- the sun in the sky-
Connected through the passing of time

Took a breath, closed my eyes
Looked inside, watching-
As time just passed me by

Here in Wonderland.

The Key of "E"

The key of "E" is
Everything
Emotions flowing
Energy
Duality
The "he," the "she,"
The key of "E" is
Everything

Shaky pieces within me
Pretending
To live peacefully
Awake but told
"Go back to sleep"
Duality says
"Let it be"
Predicting in uncertainty
Protecting from the
Fear we see
Breathing through it
Rapidly

The key of "E" is
Everything
Emotions flowing
Energy
Duality
In you and me
The key of "E" is
Everything

Continuing the same routine?
Some would say
Insanity Accepting our
Uncertainty
Noticing
Duality
It's clear to see

Come Down

When I judge you,
I, too, judge me
This energetic tethering
The fight against
Reality
Ignore the truth
In which we seek
What's happening?
We're human beings

The key of "E" is
Everything
Emotions flowing
Energy
Duality
In you and me
The key of "E" is
Everything
Duality's a tricky thing
Flowing when
You feel the sting
Aware of where
You need to be
Right here, accepting
In the stream-
Spinning
Dancing
Praying
Scream
Then
Sing

The key of "E" is
Everything
Emotions flowing
Energy
Duality
In you and me
The key of "E" is
Everything
Changes us
Serenity.

Sit Inside

Sitting inside, stuck.
Looking outside at what
Could be, should be, our dreams and desires
Sitting inside, stuck putting out the fires,
That outside distracted us from focusing on,

But
She resists to sit inside herself
Pieced together, finally, after all these years-
The tears, the fears
Have all been repressed
The mirrors.
She dare not test.
Broken puzzle pieces built her walls
Carefully protecting her deepest falls,
She resists to sit inside herself.
But
She persists to dig,
In spite of herself.

To figure it out, this Pandora's box, and settle in-
"Settle in?"
And unsettling thought...

The stagnant energy up on the shelf,
She grabs, dusts it,
Her breath fogs up,
She wipes it down-
She breathes again,
And 'round and 'round-
She resists to let herself fall down-
Again-
Those balanced walls she built around...
All those years it took, and now?

A Poetic Evolution of the Soul

Discomfort, stay here, let it be
Name it, grab it, this memory
Observe it, watch it floating by,
Release it up to Father Sky,

Connecting back down to Her roots,
To Mother Earth, your Ancestral Truths.
To not confuse their pains for Hers
This is where the Treasure's stored.

Acknowledging the strength it takes
To say
To stay inside this place

Releasing all the guilt and shame,
Sitting deep inside this pain
Accepting this is how they came,

Allow that shit to flow again.
Just let it out,
Then let it go,
This is where She really grows
Inside the vibrating
Ebb and flow

To heal her past,
That Ancestral Tree.
This can be a scary thing
Connecting in a different way
Healing wounds that try to stay
Admitting, find the inner strength she needs
To remember who's she's meant to be.

Come Down

Sitting inside.
Looking within
Allowing what's there to flow through the skin
Breathe it in
Deep
Then Let it all go
This is the
Sit inside, with it, energy flow.

Home Sweet Home

It starts in the Earth: rocks, dust, and dirt
The foundational connection
It starts in the Earth.

It builds through the bricks,
Separating *that* from *this*
The connected, but separate flow
The rooms are built through the bricks

It stands with the walls
The *lean on me* so you don't fall
The energy racing through the halls
It stands with the walls

It's decorated by the color
Personality like no other
The house is yours, embrace it,
Sister, brother,
It's decorated by the color

It breathes with the breeze
Cracked windows, flowing free
Slowly, through with ease
Accept the truth the fresh air brings
It breathes with the breeze

The view!
Look at you!
You've created something new
Put together, hard work pays off
It's You, enjoy the view

Come Down

A lifetime of sacrifices
Listening to guided advices
Paid up all your debted prices
A lifetime of sacrifices.

Now that you have it
You are just getting started
As your house becomes your home.
You are just getting started

Flowing, growing in this place
Life unfolding in each space
The rooms fill up at their own pace
Accept the messes, come what may
Flowing, growing in this place

You've been here before

Make your bed up everyday,
Decide the flow you want to take
Into the halls, the rise and falls
Support yourself against the walls and
Make your bed up everyday.

Observe the messy living room,
The need to dust, repaint, to broom
Accept the life and love inside
This Space
Create
No need to hide,
Pretending love's not here,
My dear

It is.

A Poetic Evolution of the Soul

Accept the mess
And face the fear
That this is what it comes down to

Right here-
To hide the mess, you hide your truth
Let love live,
Observe this room

Create inside the kitchen, cook
Developing your taste
Hook together all your senses
Slowly, keep at your pace
Add heat
Then cool
Repeat
Together
Create inside the kitchen, cook.

And when the house feels overwhelmed,
With mess, the clutter, and all the sounds
Crack a window, feel the breeze,
Embrace the *ease* in your *dis-ease*.
Don't run into another room
To wait it out,
Sometimes,
To prune yourself of fear,
Just allow your house to fill with air.
All it really takes, you see

Slow down,
Relax, and
Just let it be.

Enjoy the views that you create.

The Roommate

Climbing up the ladder
Avoid the incessant chatter
of your roommate, who's
living inside.

The interrupting voices,
The judgment to your choices
and theirs
So you climb, you try to hide.

The Perspiration.

To wait out all this rambling
The time that you are gambling
Your awareness you have lost
Again.

Your roommate knows no different
It is on you they imprint
But by staying on the roof
You let them win.

Come Down.
Listen.

There is not enough time
I'm tired of waiting in this line- I can't do it all
Don't run, you'll fall
Slow down
Impatience
Speed up
Clean up this mess
I'm tired
But rest
is for the wicked
No, Go
Embrace these times
It's tickin'

I'm yelling, can't you hear me?!
What?
Why am I confusing?
I just see it as it happens,
I filter through the past- then,
Protect you- by just sayin'
Everything I'm thinkin'
And you just keep on playin'
along.

You are tired.

The Confrontation.

One step
Come down
Take your time
Allow
That roommate to finish their whine.
Observe them, through love, and notice
All the time
You spend with them.

It's time to mend
To shift
To bend
The view

Advice you take from them.
Because
I mean, really,
This neurotic friend-
They just can't help it in the end.

Come Down

The Conversation.

Appreciate the efforts
The purpose
behind-
Your roommate's constant
presence-
The Chattering Mind.

Just notice the dedication, the protection, the time
Devoted to narrating everything.

Chime

Goes the bell,
It's time to dismiss
Free at last from the grips
is a friend, which at first, you might miss-
Amidst
The unknown
They were always right here
Helping you to control all the things way out there
And now
On your own
With your roommate released
You have more space
To grow
To find peace.

It's not easy.

The Tree

Mommy, do you see that little tree?
It looks like me,
So small and green!
It's shaded by that bigger tree,
Just behind it, right there!
Do you see that little tree?
Is that its mommy?
That big ole tree?

Look at that one over there!
It has no leaves,
It's big, it's bare!
Why does that one look so old,
With wrinkly bark and spots of mold?
How did that tree get so old?

Little One
Let me tell you how it goes

Like each tree
Like you
Like me
The story unfolds as the trees get old.

We all have marks, like bark, you see
Each one is different than the other,
With bended branches,
And some trees cover lots of space
Because they need it,
With little trees, protected, just beneath it.

Sharing dirt, entangled roots,
Growing upward in their own truth, Following the day and night

Soaking rays up from sky.
And as they grow, their story's told

Come Down

Lessons learned from trees are gold.

But Mom...

That fluffy tree, with pointy pines,
Look, they're all standing in straight lines. Those trees are long,
they do not whine
When the winds get strong in Wintertime.

Wow! That one's like a rainbow tree!
Covering the trailed ground, you see?
The rainbow tree, right there?
Let's stop, and take a picture please!

Then there is that fallen tree,
Right there!
It fell and now I see
The animals create a home,
So, now the tree is not alone.

That one looks just like a bridge,
It's big and round.
Down on the ground,
Connecting Earth from edge to edge.

Mommy, do you like that branchy tree?
I like the ones with pretty leaves,
Like that red tree standing there!
I wonder where it came from?
It had to come from somewhere...

Honey, we can learn a lot from them
Because like trees, we each have bends
And breaks, and mold that makes
Us each ourselves
Our stories take us all to places,
You see?
We can learn a lot from trees.

We all share dirt
Our dirt is Earth
Entangled roots that came before us
Faces toward the sun above us,
Growing, holding up our pace
Life is about creating space
For one another to grow
Protecting each other
That's how we will know

That we can all just live together
Like trees, the woods
Accept the beauty of each other.
Even if we do not get it
How they got their bumps and wrinkles
We just let it go
And be
Then sprinkle
Lots of love and loads of light
Accept the trees
Trees do not fight
See, trees don't cut each other down.

Just remember, Little One,
We, like trees, share the same ground,
We are One.

Reflections in the Puddles

There is something to be said about that feeling of highest
appreciation

Like getting a good night sleep
Or having your body feel completely rested
You've digested all of these dreams
Until finally it seems
That everything starts to make sense again,

But in a shifted way
The gifted way that you can finally breathe Into the present way
that you perceive
The days, the moments, and how they come
What's done is done. It's done.

There is something to be said about that.

It's like
Once you open up your senses
It's only then, they begin to make
Not take away

It's like
Once you allow yourself to feel it
The breeze on your skin
Nature's breath go within
It takes away the things you thought you know from way back then
And now
These senses start to mend themselves
Again

It's like
Once you open up these senses
Clearly now you see
Try to remove that doubt that's on your ceiling,
Come down with me.

.

A Poetic Evolution of the Soul

Although, it's true
There's beauty in discomfort

Or so I have been told.

Find yourself fighting to breathe,
Against the wind
This shit it getting old.

Energetically afraid to move,
To lose your balance, breath, your beat.
Because we both know when you crack it open
There's things you can't unsee.

The subtlest of movements
Your shifts
Differently

The colors all seem brighter,
The music seems to hit the center of our soul-
Every time.
Every
Time.

Forcing us to dance in the rain,
Splashing through these puddles we've been so afraid to step in,
Unsure of how deep they really are
Because just from our reflection
All we see are scars.

Don't freeze.

Breathe.

Come Down

There's beauty underneath
The reflection that we see

Breathe.

Jump in and ride the splashes that we create
From the puddles we've been so afraid
To breathe.

Enjoy the new sensations
These revelations that seem to answer all the questions
Just breathe through it, breathe deep
That's what it's all about

Dancing in the rain
Riding through the waves-
Being present in this place
Embrace

The contrast of colors that our breath has just created
The magic, the music, the movement penetrated your breath.

Come down to me.

Aho.
And so it is.

Heart Stump

Bring the heat.
Connect the breath.
Feel the red,
the orange,
the yellow flames rise into your chest.
The sweat.
Connect
to the green,
the leaves, the trees-
Release
your heart.
And breathe,
Then bridge-
Relax,
Find ease,
This is your edge.

Be cooled off
By the blue,
Refreshed by water-
The peace in you.
Dip your feet into the flow-
Then, let go,
Keep going,
The ebbs come in high
with the tide. Full Moon fury
Release, and ride
the flow back out
into the abyss where the water
meets the sky,

The mist between the blues, the greens
the grayed-flamed sunset in between.
This is where you are transformed,
From water, connected to Earth,

Come Down

Then released, into new form,
Like a gas dispersing against gravity,
This seems different from what's normally
Comfortable.
The upstream pull where the flow goes out-
Then, it keeps going.
Even without
Knowing
what will be-
No doubt-
Trust this natural process,
Breathe.

You are born of the Earth,
Your stones, the bones, the dust and dirt-
Your deep, deep roots,
You are born of the Earth-
But also a creation of the Unknown Truth-
into the dust that you breathe,
in the way you move-
into this heart space of Sacred Truth,
The bridge connecting, deeply,
Me to you.

So bring the heat,
Be forced to breathe,
Ignite those flames from underneath,
Then reconnect back to the Green-
Refreshed yourself by the river stream,
See what I mean?

Heart stump.

Sky Cave

Pressing down with all you've got
Reaching towards that mountaintop,
Heart beams out, your core, the rock

How long can you take it?

Soften
And Breathe.

The battle of this Inner Earth,
That place inside, your inner worth,
The heart, it pumps to reach that spot
That love-connected mountaintop
Experience
It's everything,
Listen to the Angels sing,
"Let Freedom Ring,"

And Breathe.

Tune in.

To battle deeper in this Cave,
The source of dirt where you were made,
Inside the Cave of Mother Earth,
That is where you find rebirth.

Stay with me.

Stay open.

Connecting opposites attract,
With breath, you feel your pulse relax,
You Inner Earth, still beating truth,
The battle to connect these two-

The Father Sky and Untouched Mother,

Come Down

Inside these caves, reveal each other

Get settled in this underground
It's in Her Caves the Father's found.

Breathe.

Allow the Yin and Yang of life
To tug and pull
To heal, bring strife
The castle of the Inner Earth
Deep inside is your rebirth.

Begin to learn to tie your truths
Lace together your deepest roots
Untie the knots right where you find them,
Relace your paths up
Do not bind them.

And breathe.

You must open up your Inner Earth,
Keep rhythm as your breath supports
You to Him up in the Sky,
Connected to the very cry
Releasing you back to the ground
Just as Mother Earth surrounds
You back to your Inner Earth
Absorbed and Quenched

Sky Cave

Rebirth

Moon Blinked

Connecting with the stones
Just step
Away
Quit looking at the mud and muck
Before the sun sets
Today

Look up,
The moon has blinked us all to think
Shove down the mud so we don't sink.

We use our breath to blow the seeds of weeds to wish our needs
For this?
Then
Shove them down so far
We miss
The opportunities
Again

Because we've been moon blinked
To think
This is life
Push on,
Push through,
Push past the
Tough to make us tougher
We say we love, we love each other

But a seed, to grow, must break-
Crack open.
Softened roots,
Reach out

Come Down

It's hard to cope when the roots can't settle,
Cannot breathe
At the cost to fill this *need*
To toughen up the ego,
See?
Moon blinked opportunity.

Rethink the way we walk through mud,
Look up and observe the sun
Move slowly, as the waters floods
Away debris that's on the path.
Allowing seeds to settle
Cast away the fear to sink.
Just sink into the soil here.
Rethink.

Then link together stepping stones
These are nature's natural bones
That build us up so we don't break,
Just take
This opportunity to make a new discovery
That things aren't always as they seem,
Debris can be
The stepping stones
Connecting us back to our bones
The truth in distant memories,
To grow, root down, then settle in

Moon blinked opportunities.

Pivot

I feel the pivot shift again
The sharped edge gets hit
It hits within
Against the solid things I know
It bumps against my totem's pole
The Spirit
Animal Integrity
This is the truth in you and me
We all are on discovery
Doing it all
For all to see
The Nature
In the things we do
It's all between
The Me and You
Our truth is set
If we'd let it be
Let go enough
Discovery

But
Bumped and bruised
And bruised to bleed
We think
We feel it
When we see
The sacrifice we've made
To be
Is really more
Than what we need
You see
The thing is

Shit

Come Down

We've lost our breath again
Released it quick when we looked in
We lost it all when we went deaf
We closed our ears
And now what's left
Not listening
The mind won't see

What's truly
Our
Discovery

Trust It

Trust is such a funny thing,
Unlearned,
We're guarded from things
Unseen

I say to you
Just trust the 'verse
You say back, out of concern
A prayer requesting advice
and change
To something else you can
relate?

Just think about that for a
second.
Take a breath and
think.

I see that way she's got me
through this
Life,
The things I've seen are true.
I've felt it, watched it slowly
vibe
Around me,
Surrounding me and you.

I can't undo my deepest
truth,
And neither, too, can you.

Nor would I ever ask that of
you.

The Father in the Sky, I feel
Him
Breathing in me winds of
change.
Heartbeat of the Mother's
hearth,
Ignites in my rebirth
Remains.

It may not look the same as
you
Have felt, or read, or
understand
Accepting you just as you are
Your breath,
Heart's journey on this land.

This.
Is your path.

This.
Is mine.

They're not always meant to
intertwine.

Cheers
To the Unknown.

Find Her

Find Her
Walking
Stalking
Carefully

Down the steps
Inside the Tree
Beneath the dirt
The hurt and sting
Above the roots,
I hear Her sing
A song that is
Familiar to me

And
For now
The sting it stops
The song begins to slowly rock
In me
That all familiar energy

You've been here before

Hidden
Beneath the bark
Down deep
I love this part
Her voice, so sweet
So innocent
Asking where I've been
I've spent
Some time away
You see

A Poetic Evolution of the Soul

I see
You have been stuck
Deeply
Rooted in this muck

Come with me
Oh, Little One
We have some work to be undone

Unleash the binds,
Release your grip,
Safely,
Hand-in-hand
We'll slip
Away
Back up the steps

Unwinding up
Down from the depths

Together,
You and I

Will change
Will grow
Will rearrange

This world.

Acknowledgements

This has always been a dream of mine to write the acknowledgements page of my first book. It is absolutely incredible to have completed this journey with you.

First and foremost, I would like to thank you for taking the time to venture on this path with me. Thank you for sharing a lifetime of energy in the making. It really is so special for me to be able to share this with you.

Ode to my husband for going on this journey with me. Healing is not easy: not for the person healing or the ones closest to that person. Thank you, Alan, for being somebody that I can open up to and for sticking with me through it all. Thank you for your encouragement to continue to heal even when it was challenging. Thank you for your patience. Thank you for your love. Thank you for seeing me.

Ellyn, thank you for intuitively reaching out to me when you did and how you did. You are a pinnacle that really helped me with this energetic shift in my life. Thank you for seeing me.

Sue, thank you for opening your home and heart to me. My journey, both on and off the mat, has been truly nourished by your light. Thank you for seeing me.

Sherri, Molly, Kristina, Theresa, and Rosaleihna, where do I begin? The experiences you have each given me to heal from the inside out is truly something beyond this world. Thank you for seeing me.

A Poetic Evolution of the Soul

To my sisters in my 200-Hour Yoga Teacher Training, every time you have shared a bit of your healing journey, it deeply resonated with me in some way. Your vulnerability has shown me that is okay to be vulnerable myself. I acknowledge the courage I see in you, and in doing that, I must also acknowledge the courage I see in myself. Thank you for letting me see you so that I may, in return, see my Self too.

Last, but not least, I want to acknowledge my family. Specifically, my children: Wyatt, Eleanor and Walter. Your unconditional love, your sparks of conversation and laughter have always been a guiding light for me. To my parents and my husband's parents, thank you for your unconditional love and support as we continue to figure out our path. To my siblings, who have journeyed with me each in their own way on this path, I send you love and light. I am forever grateful for each one of you.

Forever
in
my
heart.

Each and every one of you.

Namaste.

Made in the USA
Monee, IL
21 August 2020